A Bible Alphabet
Busy Book

*Encouraging younger children
to write about Bible stories.*

THE BANNER OF TRUTH TRUST
3 Murrayfield Road, Edinburgh EH12 6EL, UK
P.O. Box 621, Carlisle, PA 17013, USA

◆

© Alison Brown 2015

◆

ISBN: 978-1-84871-628-5

◆

Typeset in Comic Sans MS at
The Banner of Truth Trust,
Edinburgh

Printed in the USA by
Versa Press Inc.,
East Peoria, IL

◆

With thanks to Elizabeth,
who kindly used these pages in her classroom.

ark

Complete the sentences.

The people in Noah's day were very ....

God told Noah to .... an ....

The ark was made from ....

It had three floors and one ....

God brought the .... to Noah.

Two of every .... went into the ark.

The people who .... God went in too.

Everything inside the ark would be ....

Here are some words to use...

build

wood

ark

door

animals

sinful

kind

safe

believed

basket

Put in the missing vowels. (a,e,i,o,u.)

B_by Moses sl_pt _n a b_sket.
Th_ bask_t w_s m_de fr_m bulrushes.
It floated near th_ riv_r b_nk.
H_s moth_r h_d hidden him th_re.
Sh_ d_dn't want th_ wicked k_ng to
f_nd h_m.

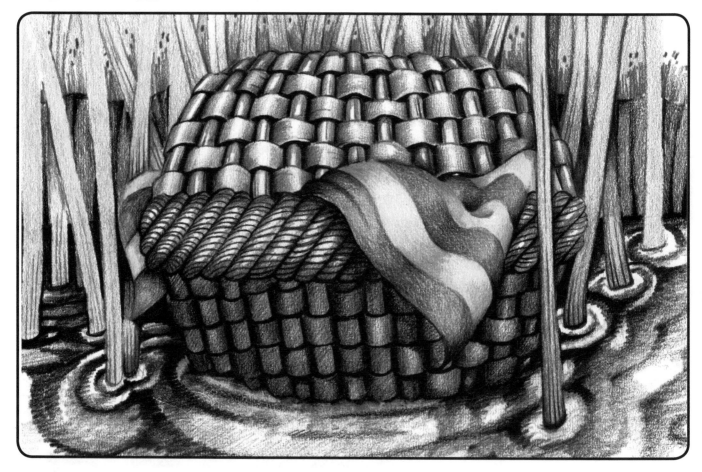

What happened to baby Moses?

....

coat

(Genesis 37:3-4)

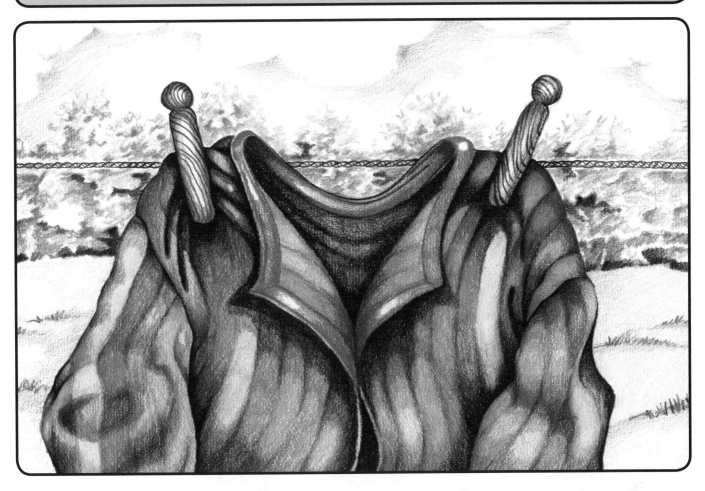

Unscramble the words to make sentences.

Joseph coat a coloured wore lovely

....

No-one coat had else a it like

....

His gave him to father it

....

He son very loved his much Joseph

....

donkey

(Numbers 22:21-35)

donkey
happen
shock
Balaam
riding
God
listen
spoke

Choose a word for each space.

The Bible tells of man called ....

Balaam had a ....

One day Balaam was .... the donkey.

Then he got a ....

The donkey .... to him!

It was .... who made it ....

He wanted Balaam to .... !

earth

Choose a word to write in each box.

tree   flowers   rock   grass   clouds

What did God say about everything he made?

....

What was the name of the first man?...............

fish

Some questions to answer...

Why was Jonah in a ship?

....

Why were all the sailors afraid?

....

What did they do to Jonah?

....

How did God keep Jonah safe?

....

Here are some words you might use...

running away

storm

fish

threw

swallow

huge

sea

giant
(1 Samuel 17:38-51)

Put in the missing vowels. (a,e,i,o,u.)

Gol_ _th w_s an _ngry gi_nt.
H_ want_d t_ f_ght G_d's peopl_.
Dav_d th_ sheph_rd b_y h_d a sl_ng.
He p_t a st_ne into th_ sl_ng.
H_ ask_d God t_ h_lp him f_ght.

What happened in the battle?

....

house

(Luke 10:38-42)

Unscramble the words to make sentences.

Mary sisters were and Martha

....

They the lived house in together same

....

Martha cook to clean liked tasty and meals

....

Mary listening Jesus to loved

....

ink

letters
safe
ink
far
God
friends
Bible

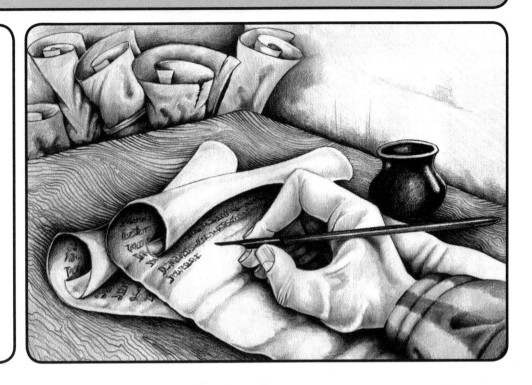

Choose a word for each space.

Paul used lots of ....

He wrote many ....

The letters were to his Christian ....

Many of them lived .... away.

Paul taught his friends about ....

His friends kept the letters ....

Some of the letters are in the .... today.

Draw your own Bible...

jail

Can you write an ending for each sentence?

Peter was put ....

But he hadn't done ....

God sent an ....

Peter's chains ....

Then the door ....

The angel led ....

These words may be useful...

jail   wrong   angel   fell   opened   anything   help   free   safely   outside

Unscramble the words to make sentences.

King very Solomon wise king a was

....

He asked him God help make good rules to

....

Some he Bible said are things written in the

....

They are book in of Proverbs the found

....

lion

Put in the missing vowels. (a,e,i,o,u.)

D_niel lov_d t_ t_lk t_ God.
Pr_ying t_ G_d was n_t all_wed.
Dani_l w_s thr_wn _nto a p_t.
It w_s f_ll _f h_ngry li_ns!
God did n_t f_rget about D_n__l.
God cl_s_d th_ l__ns' mo_ths.

What did the king think of Daniel's God?

....

manger

(Luke 2:4-7)

Joseph
room
special
baby
other
Son
stable

Choose a word for each space.

Mary's baby was born in a ....

There was no more .... in the inn.

Mary's husband was called ....

The new .... was called Jesus.

Jesus was a very .... baby.

He was different from every .... baby.

Jesus was the .... of God.

*Draw
the sky
filled
with angels...*

needle

(Acts 9:36-41)

Choose a word to write in each box.

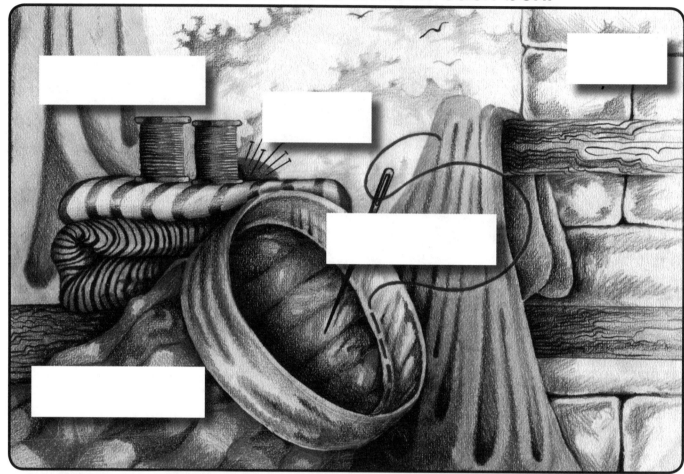

wall   needle   pins   coat   thread

Dorcas loved using a

....

She enjoyed making

....

She gave the coats to

....

Draw a colourful coat...

oil

(2 Kings 4:1-7)

Some questions to answer...

Who is the only one able to work miracles?

....

How much oil was there at the beginning?

....

When did the oil stop flowing out?

....

Who thanked God for this miracle?

....

Here are some words you might use...

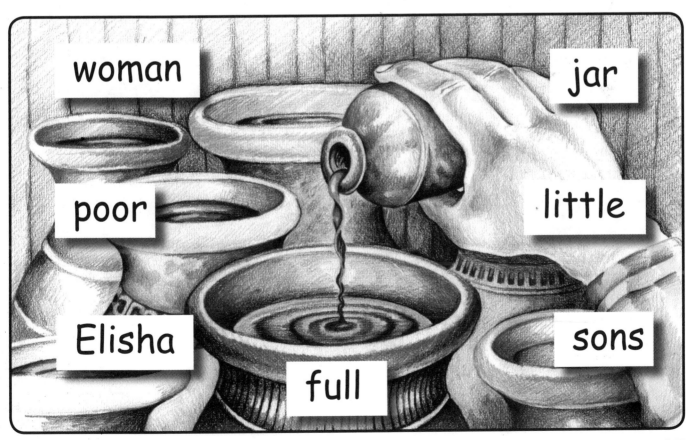

woman

jar

poor

little

Elisha

sons

full

17

picnic

(John 6:5-14)

Put in the missing vowels. (a,e,i,o,u.)

A b_y gave h_s picn_c t_ J_sus.
H_ had f_ve loav_s _nd tw_ f_sh.
Th_usands _f peopl_ w_re v_ry h_ngry.
Jes_s f_d all _f th_m!
Th_re was a l_t of f__d left ov_r!

Draw the people sharing and eating the food...

queen *(1 Kings 21:1-16)*

Unscramble the words to make sentences.

Jezebel a very queen wicked was

....

She things belong her took didn't to that

....

God everything she saw that did

....

God angry Jezebel he was punished and

....

raven

(1 Kings 17:1-6)

Can you write an ending for each sentence?

Elijah was feeling ....

He didn't have any ....

God sent ....

They brought ....

They dropped it ....

God took care ....

These words may be useful...

hungry

food

meat

bread

ravens

Elijah

beside

shepherd *(John 10:11-15)*

loves
died
sheep
people
things
shepherd
God

Choose a word for each space.

Jesus is like a ....

We are all like the ....

Like lost sheep we wander away from ....

We follow after other ....

A good shepherd really .... his sheep.

Jesus loves .... very dearly.

He loved us so much he .... for us.

Draw three sheep following a shepherd...

tent

(Genesis 12:1-8)

Some questions to answer...

What sort of home did Abraham live in?

....

Why did he not build a stone house?

....

Where was Abraham going?

....

What had God promised him?

....

Here are some words you might use...

new

land

lead

tent

travelling

unleavened bread *(Exod. 13:7-10)*

Unscramble the words to make sentences.

Sometimes ate bread Gods' unleavened people

....

It flat bread hard was

....

God's thought difficult of times people their

....

They God all for thanked help his

....

vineyard

(1 Kings 21:1-2)

Put in the missing vowels. (a,e,i,o,u.)

Nab_th own_d _ lov_ly viney_rd.
B_g juicy gr_pes gr_w on th_ vin_s.
K_ng Ah_b lived j_st n_xt d_ _r
H_ w_shed th_ v_n_yard was h_s!

Draw five big juicy grapes...

24

wall
(Nehemiah chapters 1-6)

Can you write an ending for each sentence?

The wall around Jerusalem ....

Nehemiah wanted to ....

He asked the ....

Each man worked near his own ....

Everyone worked ....

There were no...

These words may be useful...

house

fix

broken

people

hard

holes

box

(Exodus 37:1-9)

lid
tent
copy
precious
obey
priest

Choose a word for each space.

Aaron was the high ....

He worked in God's special ....

In it there was a .... golden box.

It had golden cherubims on its ....

There was a .... of God's laws in it.

God wanted his people to .... his laws.

*Draw
some priests
carrying
the golden box...*

yoke

Some questions to answer...

How do we know that Job was very rich?

....

What happened to make Job sad?

....

What did Job do then?

....

Why is God always worthy of praise?

....

Here are some words you might use...

hundred

yoke

animals

five

oxen

died

praised

zion

(Revelation 21:18-27)

Unscramble the words to make sentences.

Heaven called is Zion often

....

We in about read Bible heaven the

....

There or sun be moon heaven in will no

....

Jesus light be will the heaven in

....

Who's Who?

Noah   Naboth   Job   Mary   Aaron
Paul   Abraham   Dorcas   Jesus
God   David   Martha   God's people

1. Who built the ark? ....

2. Who used lots of ink? ....

3. Who had five hundred yoke of oxen? ....

4. Who killed the giant? ....

5. Who had a baby called Jesus? ....

6. Who made the earth? ....

7. Who was a high priest? ....

8. Who owned a vineyard? ....

9. Who ate unleavened bread? ....

10. Who was good at sewing? ....

11. Who lived in a tent? ....

12. Who is like a shepherd? ....

13. Who lived with her sister Mary? ....

Jonah Moses Jesus Peter Elijah
Jezebel Daniel Nehemiah Joseph
Elisha Balaam Solomon a little boy

14. Who slept in a basket?.....................................
15. Who wore a colourful coat?..............................
16. Who heard a donkey speak? ....
17. Who was thrown to the lions?.........................
18. Who was swallowed by a big fish? ....
19. Who mended the wall of Jerusalem?.............
20. Who was a wicked queen? ....
21. Who was fed by ravens? ....
22. Who was let out of jail by an angel? ....
23. Who gave his picnic to Jesus? ....
24. Who wrote the book of Proverbs?................
25 Who saw much oil flow from a little jar?......
26. Who will be the light in heaven? ....

My favourite Bible story in
this book is..............................

....

....

I like it best because ....

....

....

....

....

It teaches me
that God ....

....

....

....

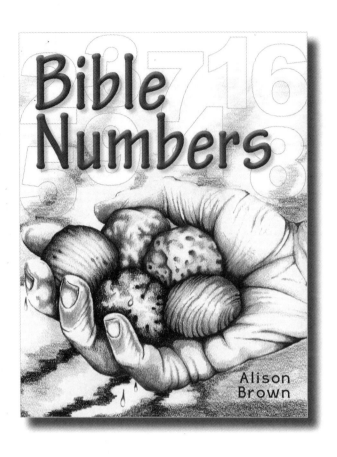

By the same author

Bible Numbers

Most young children, at some stage, are fascinated with numbers. 'Bible Numbers' introduces a dozen Bible stories for the numbers 1-12, using large, colorful illustrations, and provides a corresponding coloring page for each. At the end of the book the stories are rearranged into an order through which the gospel message is presented. Very young children may simply enjoy the number associations while the more advanced can be taught the spiritual application. A verse relevant to each Bible truth is also suggested which may prove useful as a memory verse.

32pp.

ISBN: 978-1-84871-070-2

Bible Animals

Few children can ignore an inquisitive donkey looking over a gate or the wriggling puppy they meet in the street. Animal stories also capture their attention, and are usually those with which younger children identify most readily.

Bible Animals (for ages 5+) uses a collection of animal stories drawn from Scripture, to present important, basic Bible truths. What is sin? Why did Jesus die? Why do bad things sometimes happen? Why is obedience important? These are issues about which positive God-honouring attitudes can be formed in the early years. Sharing the pages of this original book with your child provides an opportunity to begin laying these vital foundations. An animal picture to colour is provided with each lesson.

32pp.

ISBN: 978-1-84871-179-2

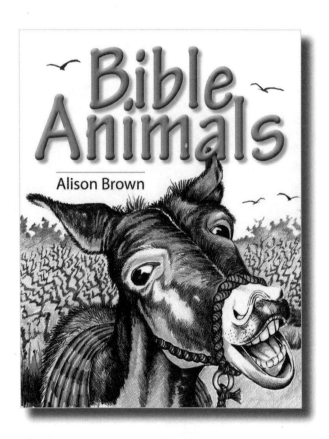